MEDIEVAL
LOVE POETRY

MEDIEVAL LOVE POETRY

EDITED BY

John Cherry

The J. Paul Getty Museum

Los Angeles

For Bridget

Frontispiece: Abduction of Ydoire, from Histoire de Charles Martel.
Tempera colors and gold on parchment. Loyset Liédet, Flemish, 1467–72.

Photography by British Museum Department of Photography
and Imaging (Saul Peckham)

First published in the United States of America in 2005 by
Getty Publications
1200 Getty Center Drive, Suite 500
Los Angeles, California 90049-1682
www.getty.edu

At Getty Publications:
Christopher Hudson, *Publisher*
Mark Greenberg, *Editor in Chief*

Library of Congress Control Number 2005923864
ISBN 0-89236-839-X
ISBN 978-0-89236-839-6

Designed and typeset in Centaur by Peter Ward
Printed in China by C & C Offset Printing Co., Ltd

CONTENTS

Gold ring set with a sapphire, inscribed inside with the figure of a lady holding a squirrel on a lead and outside with a message of love in a grammatical metaphor which continues on the inside. French, late 14th century.

Une fame nominative
A fait de moy son datiff
par la parole genitive
en depit de laccusatiff
Srs amour est infiniti[v]e
ge veu son relatiff

A nominative lady
has made me her dative
by the genitive word
despite the accusative –
love is infinitive
for her relative

INTRODUCTION

AMOR VINCIT OMNIA (love conquers all) is perhaps the world's best-known expression of love. Originally derived from the Roman writer Vergil, it was often inscribed on medieval brooches. The most famous is the one belonging to the Prioress in Chaucer's *Canterbury Tales*, who wore on her rosary:

> a broche of gold ful shene,
> On which there was first write a crowned A
> And after, Amor Vincit Omnia

This selection of medieval love poetry has two aims. The first is simply to show the charming and delightful phrases inscribed on jewellery, which explain why it was worn. These range from the very simple, such as 'Je suy vostre sans departier' (I am yours for ever) on the Fishpool brooch (p. 77), to the very complex, as on a French ring (opposite).

Images of medieval jewellery with their inscriptions, and other images of love, are here placed between series of extracts from romances – stories of medieval love and adventure. They separate the stories as flowers often divided the words in medieval inscriptions.

The second purpose of this collection is to illustrate the romances themselves. Some images show individual scenes, others give more of the narrative sequence. Brief summaries of the stories are provided at the start of each sequence.

The essence of courtly love is that a male lover serves his chosen Lady, rather than seeking to dominate her. The lover places himself humbly in the service of his lady. The ideal love should not be one-sided, and the expression of shared love is a state of joy. However, since the male lover was often of a lower social status than his beloved, such joy was often unattainable and was sometimes prevented by the haughty or fickle conduct of the lady. This self-denying service in the name of love was often carried out from afar and never consummated.

The concept of courtly love originated in Provence, in the South of France, in the twelfth century. It is not clear how and why it arose. Many reasons have been suggested, ranging from the sociological – the number of young knights compared to the number of marriageable women, or the accessibility of noble wives during their husbands' absences on crusade – to cultural factors, such as the relatively free culture of Provence at the time or the influence of Latin or Arabic literature. Whatever the exact origin (and the actual term 'courtly love' was not coined until the nineteenth century), its essential characteristic was 'the realisation that the love of women can be a precious and life enhancing experience, not gulped down to slake a moment's thirst or laid aside under the seal of marriage for every day use'. The troubadour Blondel de Nesle expressed it this way:

> Ah, God of Love, how great is your dominion! You have the power to slay lovers or to save them, giving death to one and life to others, making one man languish another laugh and sport. Me you have slain and now bring back to life, and I must worship you above everything; for you have made her my friend who was my enemy, and for this I owe you great love. Now I shall sing your praises all my life, your willing servant, glad to honour you.

A later display of how the lover was prepared to lay down his life for his beloved occurs on the fifteenth-century Shield of Parade (p. 59)

Gold inscribed ring-brooch found at Writtle, Essex,
13th century. The complete inscription reads:

✠ IEO : SUI : FERMAIL : PUR : GAR : DER : SEIN
✠ KE : NU : SVILEIN : NIMETTE : MEIN

I am the brooch to guard the breast
So that no churl may put his hand there.

where the lover, about to fight in a tournament, sees his future choice between love of the lady or his death.

The concept of courtly love underlies the romances chosen here. The story of Tristan and Isolt is well known to us through the music of Richard Wagner. In origin the story goes back to Celtic sources: the French and German versions set the story in Cornwall, Ireland and Brittany. The tiles from Chertsey Abbey illustrate the version by Thomas. Although found at an Abbey, they were designed to floor an English royal palace, possibly Westminster Palace. The illustrations on these tiles convey a vivid sense of the feelings of the participants, as when the barons lament their sons (p. 17), and capture essential moments in the story, as when Isolt signals to Tristan (p. 23).

The romance of Lancelot and that of Gawain and the Green Knight are both set in the surroundings of the court of King Arthur. Lancelot was written by Chretien de Troyes, a great French writer of romance, in the second half of the twelfth century, so it is a late addition to the group of Arthurian tales. Lancelot tells of the struggles the hero has to overcome to rescue Guinevere, Arthur's queen, from her captor. We do not know who wrote the poem Sir Gawain and the Green Knight, but since it is contained in a manuscript with other poems such as that entitled Pearl, it is assumed that the same poet wrote it in the 1340s.

The Chatelaine of Vergi is one of the most beautiful of the late medieval stories of love. Written before 1288 in a Franco-Burgundian dialect, it is set in Burgundy and the poet may have reflected actual events. Although at least six ivory caskets exist which show this story, it is not commonly illustrated elsewhere.

The Romance of the Rose, composed by Guillaume de Lorris in the 1230s and continued by Jean de Meung some forty years later, was one of the most popular poems of the Middle Ages. Written in the form of an allegory, it proved to be one of the most popular expressions of fine aristocratic love. It is the story of a dreamer's quest for his beloved. She is never given human shape, but her heart and innermost self are visualized as a rosebud. The Rose is imprisoned in the castle of Jealousy (p. 89) and is only released when Venus, the goddess of love, has shot her fiery brand, after which the lover finally attains the Rose.

Scenes of courtly love were illustrated on rich and luxurious objects, some of which were gifts of love and others, no doubt, held the gold jewels that held memories of love. Ivory, the tusk of elephants, was used to carve the sides of caskets as well as writing tablets, mirror cases and combs. Some caskets, such as those displaying the story of the Chatelaine of Vergi, attempt to show the whole story within the five available panels, while other caskets, known as 'Romance' caskets, show individual scenes from different romances as well as other unrelated scenes. One 'Romance' casket (p. 51) has the Assault on the Castle of Love on the lid, and scenes from Lancelot and Tristan on the sides. A favourite scene for individual writing tablets and mirror cases was the scene from Tristan of King Mark in the tree, above the pool (p. 25).

The Assault on the Castle of Love, in which the castle is attacked by knights and defended by beautiful ladies wielding roses, has no literary source and is not related to the Romance of the Rose, although a castle (p. 78) plays a prominent part in that story. Such images reflect actual 'sieges' of 'castles of love' that took place at festivals in the thirteenth century. The concept of the feminine defence of the castle using delightful objects and flowers may refer to the defence of chastity, but it also provides a vision of the way in which love conquers all.

THE TROUBADOUR

Oh God, why am I not a starling
who flies through the air
so that in the depth of the night
I may come to her?
Worthy, joyful lady,
Your lover is dying!
I fear my heart will melt
if it continues thus.
Lady, for your love
I join hands and worship you.
Gentle body with fresh skin,
What grief you bring me!

Two lovers on an enamelled Limoges casket.
French, late 12th century.

TRISTAN AND ISOLT (1)

TRISTAN is a nephew of Mark, king of Cornwall. He goes to his uncle's court at Tintagel where he kills the Irish giant Morholt, who has come to claim the sons of the barons of Cornwall as tribute. Tristan then goes to Ireland to recover from his wounds where he is nursed by Isolt, daughter of the king of Ireland. Mark then decides he wishes to marry Isolt and sends Tristan back to ask the Irish king for her hand in marriage. Isolt's mother prepares a magic love potion for Mark and Isolt, but during their journey to Cornwall Brangwain, Isolt's attendant, gives the love potion to Tristan and Isolt by mistake. Mark and Isolt marry, but Mark suspects Isolt of infidelity with Tristan and hides in a tree to observe their meeting. They see the reflection of Mark's face in a pool beneath the tree and are thereby alerted to conceal their love. Tristan goes off to pursue adventures in Brittany and there marries the daughter of the Duke, who is also called Isolt. When he is mortally wounded, he summons Isolt, wife of Mark, as the only person who can cure him. As a signal, the boat carrying Isolt from Cornwall is to bear white sails but, if Isolt is not aboard, the sails are to be black. The boat bringing Isolt comes bearing white sails but is becalmed. Meanwhile Tristan's wife Isolt of Brittany, who has overheard his instructions, tells her husband that the sails are black, and he dies in despair. Isolt arrives to find Tristan dead. She kisses him and dies, holding him in her arms.

Tile from Chertsey Abbey showing Tristan harping
before King Mark. Late 13th century.

Then Tristan took the harp and sang so well that the barons
softened as they heard, and King Mark marvelled at the harper
from Lyonesse . . .

The King said: 'Son, blessed be the master that taught thee,
and blessed be thou of God: for God loves good singers. Their
voices and the voice of the harp enter the souls of men and wake
dear memories and cause them to forget many a mourning and
many a sin. For our joy did you come to this roof, stay near us
a long time, friend.'

And Tristan answered: 'Very willingly will I serve you sire,
as your harper, huntsman and your liege.'

TRISTAN AND ISOLT (2)

There were also comen the noblest ladies with their sons, and
they were about to be chosen that should go as tribute to
Ireland. All made great lamentation of their sorrow and
misery; each feareth for their son lest his lot should
come up . . . Much dole and dolorous shame was it
that boys of such worship born were given into such
thraldom and servage. Lord God, long suffering art
thou that endurest such deeds! Have pity of their
grievous distress! Noble men wept, women wailed
and shrieked, children cried.

Tile from Chertsey Abbey showing
the barons of Cornwall lamenting for
their sons. Late 13th century.

TRISTAN AND ISOLT (3)

Then was Tristan right wroth and brandished his
sword and smote down on Morholt's head betwixt shield
and helm, and carf in sunder the strap and the helms
brim and a quarter of the shield with its glittering gold
and gems, and shore the hauberk from his arm and so
much of the flesh as the sword took, and clave in under
the saddle bow, and pierced more than a span deep into
his horse croup: and this stroke had gained more, had
his shield been longer.

Tristan at battle, from Roman de Bon Chevalier Tristan.
Tempera colours and gold on parchment. French, Paris, c. 1320–40.

TRISTAN AND ISOLT (4)

Brangwain came upon them. She saw them gazing at each other in silence as though ravished and apart: she saw before them the pitcher standing there: she snatched it up and cast it into the shuddering sea and cried aloud: 'Cursed be the day I was born and cursed the day that I first trod this deck. Isolt, my friend, and Tristan, you, you have drunk death together.'

Ivory casket. Brangwain
giving the love-potion to Tristan and Isolt.
Cologne, early 13th century.

TRISTAN AND ISOLT (5)

Isolt purposed that he should bear her from the boat where she was to be carried across the water, and then would she tell him a secret thing. He took good heed by his troth that he should be there on the day assigned, all so disguised that no man knew him. His visage was all stained with yellow colour, and he was in a foul woollen kirtle and an old cloak over him. The queen on the other side of the river entered within a barge: she made a sign then unto Tristan.

Tile from Chertsey Abbey showing Isolt signalling to Tristan. Late 13th century.

TRISTAN AND ISOLT (6)

The King, who was up in the tree, had seen their meeting clearly and heard all they had said. The pity which filled him was so great that he could not for all the world hold back his tears; he was grief-stricken, and he began to hate the dwarf of Tintagel . . . The King climbed down from the tree thinking in his heart that he would now believe his wife and not the barons, who were trying to make him believe things which he knew were untrue and which he had proved to be false.

King Mark hiding in the tree with his head reflected in the water below, from an ivory casket. Paris, late 14th century.

TRISTAN AND ISOLT (7)

While they sailed gladly, the heat waxed and the wind fell that
they might not sail. Full soft and smooth was the sea. Nor
here nor there their ship stirred save as the wave drew it . . .
Isolt was tormented sore thereby: she perceived the land
she had coveted, but might not attain to it. Well nigh she
died of her longing. Within the ship they desired land,
but the wind blew ever so softly. Oft Isolt called herself
wretched. They wished the ship at the strand, but they
saw it no more.

Tile from Chertsey Abbey showing
Isolt voyaging to nurse Tristan.
Late 13th century.

27

JEWELS OF LOVE

I know of a beauty, a beryl most bright,
As lovely to look on as silver-foiled sapphire,
As gentle as jasper a-gleam in the light,
As true as the ruby, or garnet in gold.
Like onyx she is, esteemed in the height;
A diamond of worth when she's dressed for the day;
Like coral her lustre, like Caesar or knight;
Like emerald at morning, this maiden has might.
My precious red stone, with the power of a pearl,
I picked for her prettiness, excellent girl!

Gold brooch set with rubies
and sapphires and inscribed:
IO SUI ICI EN LIU DAMI AMO
(I am here in place of a lover, love).

LANCELOT (1)

King Arthur's Queen Guinevere is captured by Melagaunt, a prince of Gorre – a land from which no stranger returns. Arthur's knights Kay and Gawain set out to recover her. They meet an unknown knight who must adopt the humiliating pose of travelling in a cart. This is none other than Lancelot. To reach Gorre, Lancelot has to cross a raging torrent over a bridge made of a sword. Eventually he kills Melagaunt and rescues the queen.

> The knight prepared himself as best
> He could to cross the chasm
> And surprised them exceedingly
> By removing the armour from his feet and hands –
> In the extreme pain he caused him
> And in great distress he crossed,
> Wounding his hands, knees and feet.
> But Love, which led and guided him,
> Comforted and healed him at once
> And made his suffering a pleasure.

Scene from an ivory casket showing the
knight crossing the sword bridge.
Paris, late 14th century.

LANCELOT (2)

She welcomed him out of love;
But if she had strong love for him,
He felt a hundred thousand times for her.
For love in other hearts was as nothing
Compared to the love he felt in his.
Love took root in his heart,
And was so entirely there
That little was left for other hearts.

The first kiss between Lancelot and Guinevere.
From the Lancelot-Graal manuscript,
Artois or Flanders, *c.* 1320.

JEWELS OF LOVE

A lover is permitted to receive from her partner these
gifts: a napkin, hair-bands, gold or silver circlet, brooch,
mirror, belt, purse, tassel, comb, gauntlets, gloves, ring,
jewel-box, picture, bowl, vessels, plates and a pennant for
remembrance; and in general a lover will be able to accept
from her partner any small gift which can be useful for
adornment of the body or cultivation of appearance, or
which can serve as a remembrance of a partner, always
provided that in accepting the gift she is seen to be free
of all suspicion of greed.

Gold padlock found with the Fishpool hoard and inscribed
DE TOUT MON CUER (with all my heart). 15th century.

SIR GAWAIN AND THE GREEN KNIGHT (1)

THE GREEN KNIGHT appears in Camelot, King Arthur's court, on New Year's day. He invites any knight to strike him an axe blow, on condition that he will stand a return blow on the same day a year hence. Gawain accepts and strikes off the head of the Green Knight.

The following year, Gawain sets off to find the Green Knight. He arrives at a castle near the Green Chapel and is invited to stay there until New Year's day, with the agreement that Gawain and his mysterious host shall each give the other whatever he receives. While his host is away hunting, the lady of the castle makes love to Gawain and, on the third day, she gives him her girdle which preserves the wearer from wounds. Each evening Gawain gives the kisses that he has received to his host, but he conceals the gift of the magical girdle.

On New Year's day the Green Knight appears and wounds Gawain before revealing that he is Gawain's mysterious host, and that he had agreed with his wife to tempt Gawain. The Green Knight claims he would not have harmed Gawain if he had not concealed the gift of the girdle. Gawain returns to Arthur's court, bearing the girdle as a sign of his shame. King Arthur's knights agree to wear a bright green belt for Gawain's sake.

To the high fields he hurried with hunting horn then.
Just as daylight was dawning – it dimly arose –
That host was up high on his horse, with his men.
The helpers harnessed their hounds in matched pairs,
And unlocked the gates, unloosing those dogs
By the blowing of bugles: three bold, single notes.
Those dogs raised a din not diminished until
They were scolded, restrained by the shouts of the men:
A hundred brave hunters, I've heard every one renowned.
The servants, staying still,
At last unleashed each hound.
From bugles, sharp and shrill,
The forest filled with sound.

Two hunting scenes, details from around the handle
of a boxwood gittern, a medieval musical instrument
resembling a guitar. Early 14th century.

SIR GAWAIN
AND THE GREEN KNIGHT (2)

Then was Gringolet girded with a great, stately saddle,
Aglow with the glints of a good golden fringe.
For the nonce studded newly with nails everywhere,
The rich bridle was barred with the brightest of gold.
The shimmering skirts and the shining poitrel
Were accorded with the caparison, crupper and saddle bows –
All in red well arrayed, and with rich golden studs
That would glisten and glint like the gleams of the sun.

Scene of the arming of Sir Geoffrey Luttrell,
from the Luttrell Psalter. English, *c.* 1325–35.

SIR GAWAIN
AND THE GREEN KNIGHT (3)

For the head in his hand he holds out to all,
To the dais directs it, to dear nobles there;
It lifts up its lids and looks about,
And not waiting, says wonderful words, as you'll hear:
'Be prepared to perform as you've promised, Gawain.
You must ferret with faith till you find me at last,
Just as here in this hall all have heard you now pledge
To the Green Chapel's chambers I charge you to go.'

Gawain and the Green Knight.
English, 1400–1410.

SIR GAWAIN
AND THE GREEN KNIGHT (4)

Again to Sir Gawain the girdle she offered.
When he granted, she gladly gave him that belt.
For her sake, she beseeched he conceal the gift
From her lord. He allowed it at last; he agreed
To be loyal to the lady; his lips would remain
Sealed tight.
Gawain, again and again,
Thanks showered, showed delight.
That loving Lady then
A good kiss gave her knight.

The wife of the Green Knight
visits Gawain in his bedchamber.
English, 1400–1410.

SIR GAWAIN
AND THE GREEN KNIGHT (5)

The king and the court brought comfort to him.
They laughed out right loud, and at last all agreed —
Every lady and lord who belonged to the Table —
That a baldric be borne by the brotherhood's men,
A silk band wrapped about of bright, glowing green
For the sake of that shining knight, showing respect.
Thus that token the Table took as a sign
Of renown; and that knight ever knew honor —
In our richest romance this is written down well.

Gawain returns to King Arthur's court.
English, 1400–1410.

JEWELS OF LOVE

Faireste of faire. O Lady myn, Venus
Doughter to Jove and spouse of Vulcanus,
Thou glader of the mount of Citheroun
For thilke love thou haddest to Adoun
Have pitee of my bittre teres smerte
And take myn humble preyer at thyn herte.

Seal matrix set with stone (sard) intaglio showing
Venus holding a bearded mask in front of a statue of
a youth, and the inscription IE SUI SEL DAMUR LEL
(I am a seal of loyal love). 14th century.

THE GAMES OF LOVE (1)

A broche, gold and asure,
In whiche a ruby set was lyk an herte,
Criseyde hym yaf, and stak it on his sherte.

Trewe loue among men that most is of lette [late]
In hates, in hodes, in porses is sette.
Trewe loue in herbers [arbours] spryngeth in May,
Bote trewe loue of herte went is away

The offering of a heart (left) and a purse (right).
From the Alexander Romance manuscript created under
the direction of Jean de Grise, Bruges, 1344.

49

THE GAMES OF LOVE (2)

A fantastic castle was built and garrisoned with dames and damsels and their waiting women, who, without help of men, defended it with all possible prudence. Now this castle was fortified on all sides with skins of vair and sable, sendals, purple cloths, samites, precious tissues, scarlet, brocade of Bagdad, and ermine. What shall I say of the golden coronets, studded with chrysolites and jacinths, topaz and emeralds, pearls and pointed headgear and all manner of adornments wherewith the ladies defended their heads from the assaults of the beleaguerers. For the castle itself must needs be assaulted; and the arms and the engines wherewith men fought against it were apples and dates and muscat-nuts, tarts and pears and quinces, roses and lilies and violets, and vases of balsam or ambergris or rosewater, amber, camphor, cardomums, cinnamon, cloves and all manner of flowers and spices that are fragrant to smell or fair to see.

The lid of an ivory casket,
showing the Assault on the Castle of Love.
Paris, 14th century.

THE GAMES OF LOVE (3)

A very large fountain, carried on their shoulders by twelve men, on the foot of which are six knights attacking the castle . . . In the middle of the castle, in the fashion of a great tower with several turrets, and the castle stands on a high green hill; The hill has battlemented barbicans, and above on the battlements of the castle are women who hold maces and shields and defend the castle . . . At the bottom is a large enamel with a knight and his lady in a blue pavilion. The knight holds a heart in his right hand and the lady a little dog in her left hand. The enamel of the cover, also blue, shows a knight holding a heart in his left hand talking to the lady beside him.

The Assault on the Castle of Love,
from the Luttrell Psalter. English, *c.* 1325–35.

THE GAMES OF LOVE (4)

A beauty white as whale's bone;
A golden bead, shining alone;
A turtle my heart is fixed upon,
Earth's truest thing!
Her gaiety will not be gone
While I can sing.

When blisses on this beauty pour,
Of all this world I ask no more
Than be alone with her and draw
No word of strife.
I blame a lovely woman for
My woes in life.

Ivory writing tablet showing a game of forfeits.
French, 14th century.

THE GAMES OF LOVE (5)

In Maytime in the merry dawn
The leaves are bright on hill and lawn
And beasts to joy inclined.
On branches gorgeous blossoms grow,
And wanton folk a-wooing go:
I have it much in mind.
I cannot think of finer flowers
Than brilliant ladies in their bowers
By yearning love confined.
Such wonderful girls are in the West:
The one I worship is the best
From Ireland into Ind.

Young men and women outdoors,
from Historia de duobus amantibus.
Tempera colours and gold on parchment.
French, *c.* 1460–70.

THE GAMES OF LOVE (6)

Ah, God of Love, how great is your dominion! You have the power to slay lovers or to save them, giving death to one and life to others, making one man languish, another laugh and sport. Me you have slain and now brought back to life, and I must worship you above everything; for you have made her my friend who was my enemy, and for this I owe you great love. Now I shall sing your praises all my life, your willing servant, glad to honour you.

Shield of Parade, painted with a scene showing a lover dedicating himself to his lady. Death stands behind him, and above his head a scroll reads: VOUS OU LA MORT (You or Death).

THE GAMES OF LOVE (7)

Je ne prise point tels baisiers
Qui sont donnés par contenance,
Ou par maniere d'acointance:
Trop de gens en sont parçonniers.

Mais savez vous lesquels sont chiers?
Les privés, venans par plaisance;
Tous autres ne sont, sans doutance,
Que pour festier estrangiers.
Je ne prise point tels baisiers!

I think nothing of such kisses
As are given by convention,
As a matter of politeness:
Far too many people share them.

Do you know the ones I value?
Secret ones, bestowed in pleasure;
All the rest are doubtless nothing
But a way of greeting strangers.
I think of nothing but such kisses!

A kiss, from the Talbot leather casket.
Northern France or Flanders, late 14th century.

JEWELS OF LOVE

Dedens mon Livre de Pensée,
J'ay trouvé escripvant mon cueur
Le vray histoire de douleur,
De larmes toutes enluminée.

In my book of thoughts
I have found written on my heart
The true history of sadness
All illuminated with tears.

The two sides of a gold heart-shaped jewel found at Rocklea Sands, Poole,
showing tears on one side and on the other an ivy leaf, within the legend
TRISTES EN PLESIRE (sadness in pleasure).

THE CHATELAINE OF VERGI (1)

THE CHATELAINE OF VERGI, a niece of the Duke of Burgundy, is married and having a secret affair with a knight at her uncle's court. She signals to the knight that it is safe to visit her when she sends out to him a dog. The Duke's wife, the Duchess, is also attracted to the knight. She tries to seduce him and, when refused, tells her husband that the knight has tried to seduce her. When the Duke threatens the knight with execution, the knight reveals his secret affair to the Duke. The Duke witnesses a meeting of the lovers and promises the knight not to reveal their secret. The Duchess, annoyed that the knight has not been punished, refuses to sleep with the Duke, who tells her the story of the knight and his niece. At a ball, the Duchess compliments the niece on her ability to train dogs. The Chatelaine, believing she has been publicly disgraced and that the knight has betrayed her, kills herself. The knight discovers her body, hears an account of her humiliation and death, and stabs himself. On finding their bodies, the Duke takes the sword and kills his wife.

> And to enjoy their love, they devised for the Knight to
> come always into an orchard, when she should appoint,
> and in nowise stir from one corner of it until he had seen
> a little dog cross the orchard. Then, without tarrying,
> might he come to her chamber and know well that he
> would find his lady alone.

The Chatelaine of Vergi and her dog, from the left side of
the lid of an ivory casket. French, 14th century.

THE CHATELAINE OF VERGI (2)

'Then hate this one', said she (and she named unto him
the Knight), 'who has ceased not the whole day long to
pray me for my love. Longtime, said he, had he thought
on this, but ne'er had he dared utter it. And I was
resolved, good sire, to make it known unto you, for it may
be true that he has longwhiles thought on this, for never
we have heard that he loves another. So I pray you, in
requital, to protect your honour, since you know this to
be right.'

The Duchess denounces the Knight to the Duke,
from the right side of an ivory casket lid.
French, 14th century.

THE CHATELAINE OF VERGI (3)

They were come into the garden, and there the Duke
waited not long ere he saw his niece's little dog come to
the corner of the orchard, where it found the knight, who
made much ado over it . . . And the Duke, who was
crouching down quite close to them at the door, heard all,
and so well were the voice and the manner of his niece

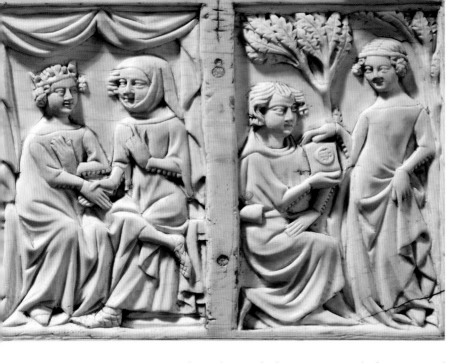

The Duke sees the lovers meet, reveals their story and
summons the Lady. From the back of an ivory casket.
French, 14th century.

known to him, that no longer was he in doubt, and
determined that that which the Duchess had told him was
false, and greatly was he pleased, for now he saw well that
the Knight wronged him not in such manner as he had
had suspicion of him.

THE CHATELAINE OF VERGI (4)

On the occasion of a court dance called a carole, the
Duchess says to the Duke's niece: 'Chatelaine . . . you
have as an acquaintance a handsome and brave lover'.

'Of a truth, my lady . . . I desire not to have for lover
any one who may not be in all things to mine honour,
and to that of my lord'.

'Right well do I grant you this', said the Duchess,
'but you are a clever mistress to have learnt how to train
the little dog'.

The carole, from the side of an ivory casket.
French, 14th century.

THE CHATELAINE OF VERGI (5)

When I freely gave him my love, I said to him, that
whensoever he made known our love, he would lose me . . .
I pray to God to send me death, and that as, in very
truth, I have loved him who has so repaid me, he may
have pity on my soul . . . and I pardon him. And my
death is sweet since it comes from him, and when I have
in remembrance his love, it grieves me not to die for him.

The Chatelaine dies and the Knight kills himself (left).
The Duke enters and draws out the sword, then goes to the ball.
From the front of an ivory casket. French, 14th century.

Then was the Duke mad with rage. And straightway he
entered the chamber and drew out of the body of the
knight the sword with which he had killed himself . . .

THE CHATELAINE OF VERGI (6)

And forthwith the Duke went to the Duchess, and made good his promise to her, and without uttering a word, struck her on the head with the naked sword that he held, so wrathful was he. And the Duchess died . . .

And on the morrow, the Duke caused the lovers to be buried in one grave, and the Duchess in another place. And forthwith he went on a crusade beyond the sea from whence he returned not . . .

The Duke stops the dance and kills the Duchess.
From the side of an ivory casket. French, 14th century.

JEWELS OF LOVE

Have all my hert and be in peace
And think I love you fervently
For in good faith, it is no lese
I would thee wyst as well as I,
That my love will not cease
Have mercy on me as thee best may
Have all my hert and be in peace.

Heart-shaped gold brooch found with the Fishpool hoard,
with the inscription JE SUY VOSTRE SANS DE PARTIER
(I am yours forever). English, 15th century.

77

THE ROMANCE OF THE ROSE (1)

THE ROMANCE OF THE ROSE is an allegorical presentation of courtly love. The story is in the form of a dream in which the lover wakes and visits a garden. He is invited to enter by Idleness. Inside he sees the Rose and falls in love with it. Jealousy constructs a great castle around the rose bed. This castle is attacked and the Rose finally attained.

> Calm and serene, and bright and sweet,
> Was that spring morning, as my feet
> Along the river bank I bent,
> Light-hearted, heedless where I went,
> And hearkening, as it rolled along,
> The stream's unending murmur-song.

The lover sleeps, dresses and goes out into the garden.
South Netherlands or Bruges, c. 1490–1500.

THE ROMANCE OF THE ROSE (2)

Short space my feet had traversed ere
A garden spied I, great and fair,
The which a castled wall hemmed round,
And pictured thereupon I found
Full many a figure rich and bright
Of colour, and how each one hight
Clear writ beneath it.

The lover is admitted to the garden, from Roman de la Rose.
Tempera colours and gold on parchment. French, Paris, *c.* 1405.

THE ROMANCE OF THE ROSE (3)

I stood awhile, as one entranced,
To watch how wondrously they danced,
Till tripped across the sward to me
A winsome dame, hight Courtesy.
Past power of words I found her fair,
Bewitching, bright and debonair.
(May God preserve her life from harm)
At once with voice that seemed to charm
All fear away, she cried: Fair sir,
Wilt thou not deign thy foot to stir
In jocund dance?

The lover (far left) is invited by a lady to join the dance.
South Netherlands or Bruges, *c.* 1490–1500.

THE ROMANCE OF THE ROSE (4)

            I espied
With joy its lovely petals, which
Kind Nature's hand had dyed with rich
Deep crimson hue. Its perfect leaves
Were formed of two quadruple sheaves,
Which side by side stood firm and fair
With stalk strong grown enough to bear
The full-grown bloom which did not bend
Or languish, but most sweetly spend
Its fragrance on the air around,
And wrapt my senses in profound
Yet soft delight.

The lover is led to the Rose.
South Netherlands or Bruges, *c.* 1490–1500.

THE ROMANCE OF THE ROSE (5)

Love then from forth his alm'ner drew
A little key, well-wrought anew
Of thrice refinèd gold, and said:
'This to thy heart my hand must wed;
To its safe keeping I confide
My jewels; ne'er hath it belied
My perfect trust. It doth possess
Great virtue, and in size though less
Than thy small finger, yet, 'tis strong;
The name that to it doth belong
Is: Mistress of my jewels rare.'

Love locks the heart of the lover.
French, Paris, c. 1380.

THE ROMANCE OF THE ROSE (6)

So now that Jealousy at last
Hath seen Fair-Welcome, hard and fast,
Within this prison tower immured,
Boundeth her heart, of peace assured
Against all violence and wrong,
Misdoubting nought that castle strong.
No longer hath she cause to fear
Lest rude marauders come anear
Roses or rosebuds, they repose
Safely within that high-built close.

The castle of Jealousy.
South Netherlands or Bruges, *c.* 1490–1500.

THE ROMANCE OF THE ROSE (7)

Then Beauty gave
In secret that my heart did crave
The precious Rosebud, which I took
With rapture while my being shook
With tremulous joy. Couched on the grass,
New sprung, we saw the moments pass
In soft content; our coverlet
Of fragrant rose-leaves made, while met
Our lips in fond embrace.

The lover attains the Rose.
French, 1487-95.

JEWELS OF LOVE

Of smal coral aboute hir arm she bar
A peire of bedes, gauded al with grene
And ther-on heng a broche of gold ful shene,
On which there was first write a crowned A
And after, Amor Vincit Omnia.

Gold brooch inscribed AMOR VINCIT OMNIA
(love conquers all). English, 14th century.

TEXT SOURCES AND FURTHER READING

Most of the romances were originally composed in medieval French. Scenes are described here using English translations drawn from a miscellany of translators and styles (selected from the texts listed below). The best general introductions are by Michael Camille, *The Medieval Art of Love* (Laurence King, 1998), Malcolm Jones, *The Secret Middle Ages* (Alan Sutton, 2002) and D. D. R. Owen, *Noble Lovers* (Phaidon Press, 1975). All have good bibliographies. Also recommended is Sarah Kay, *The Romance of the Rose* (Grant and Cutler, 1995). For secular art and craftsmanship, see John Cherry, *Medieval Decorative Art* (British Museum Press, 1991) and *Goldsmiths* in the Medieval Craftsmen series (British Museum Press, 1992). For ivories, see Peter Barnet (ed.), *Images in Ivory: Precious Objects of the Gothic Age* (Detroit Institute of Arts, 1997).

TEXTS OF ROMANCES AND POETRY

Andreas Capellanus on Love, translated by R. G. Walsh: Duckworth & Co., 1982, p. 269

Charles d'Orleans, by Enid McLeod: Chatto & Windus, 1969, p. 306 (reprinted by permission of The Random House Group Ltd)

'The Chatelaine of Vergi', in *Aucassin and Nicolette and Other Tales*, translated by Pauline Matarasso: Penguin Books, 1971

The Chatelaine of Vergi, translated by Alice Kemp Welch: Chatto & Windus, 1908, pp. 20, 24, 34–6, 47, 51 and 55–6

'The Knightes Tale', in *Complete Works of Geoffrey Chaucer*, edited by W. W. Skeat: Oxford University Press, 1912, lines 2221–6

Lancelot or The Knight of the Cart (Le Chevalier de la Charrette), by Chretien de Troyes, edited and translated by William W. Kibler: Garland Publishing, 1981, p. 131, lines 3094–7 and 3110–16 and p. 195, lines 4661–8

Medieval English Verse, translated by Brian Stone: Penguin Classics, 1964, Harley Lyrics 87 (1 and 5), 88 and 90 (1) (© Brian Stone, 1964, reproduced by permission of Penguin Books Ltd)

Noble Lovers, by D. D. R. Owen: Phaidon Press, 1975, p. 28 (© 1975 by Phaidon Press, www.phaidon.com)

Penguin Book of French Verse, edited by Brian Woledge: Penguin Books, 1961, vol. 1, p. 298 (reprinted with permission of the estate of Professor Brian Woledge)

Rolandino of Padua, in *A Medieval Garner*, translated by G. G. Coulton: Constable & Co., 1910, pp. 268–9

The Romance of the Rose, translated by F. S. Ellis: J. M. Dent, 1900, lines 123–9, 136–43, 809–19, 1730–41, 2081–91, 4219–28 and 4276–85

The Romance of the Rose by Guillaume de Loris and Jean de Meung, translated by Charles Dahlberg: Princeton University Press, 1971

The Romance of Tristan: The Tale of Tristan's Madness by Beroul, translated by Alan S. Fedrick: Penguin Classics, 1970, pp. 52–3 (© Alan S. Fedrick, 1970, reproduced by permission of Penguin Books Ltd)

The Romance of Tristram and Ysolt by Thomas of Britain, translated by Roger Sherman Loomis: Columbia University Press, 1951, pp. 60–61, 71–2, 163 and 282 (© 1951 Columbia University Press, reprinted with permission of the publisher)

Secular Lyrics of the Fourteenth and Fifteenth Centuries, edited by R. H. Robbins: Clarendon Press, 1952, nos 135 and 173

'Sir Gawain and the Green Knight', in *Complete Poems of the Pearl Poet*, translated and edited by Casey Finch: University of California Press, 1993, lines 444–51, 597–604, 1136–49, 1860–69 and 2513–21 (© 1993 The Regents of the University of California)

Songs of the Troubadours, translated by Anthony Bonner: George Allen & Unwin, 1973, pp. 87–9

Tristran and Iseult rendered into English, by Hilaire Belloc: George Allen & Co., 1913, pp. 13 and 48–9

'Troilus and Criseyde', in *Complete Works of Geoffrey Chaucer*, edited by W. W. Skeat: Oxford University Press, 1912, Book 3, lines 1370–72

Verses in Sermons, edited by S. Wenzel: Medieval Academy of America, 1978, pp. 159–60

ILLUSTRATION REFERENCES

Photographs © The Trustees of the British Museum, Department of Prehistory and Europe (PE), courtesy of the Department of Photography and Imaging, unless otherwise noted.